Primary Sources of Westward Expansion

Lewis and Clark and Exploring the Louisiana Purchase

Alicia Z. Klepeis

Cavendish
Square

New York

Published in 2018 by Cavendish Square Publishing, LLC
243 5th Avenue, Suite 136, New York, NY 10016

Copyright © 2018 by Cavendish Square Publishing, LLC

First Edition

Library of Congress Cataloging-in-Publication Data
Names: Klepeis, Alicia, 1971-
Title: Lewis and Clark and exploring the Louisiana Purchase / Alicia Z. Klepeis.
Description: New York : Cavendish Square Publishing, [2018] |
Series: Primary sources of westward expansion | Includes bibliographical references and index.
Identifiers: LCCN 2016054484 (print) | LCCN 2016054945 (ebook) |
ISBN 9781502626394 (library bound) | ISBN 9781502626332 (E-book)
Subjects: LCSH: Lewis and Clark Expedition (1804-1806)--Juvenile literature. |
West (U.S.)--Discovery and exploration--Juvenile literature.
Classification: LCC F592.7 .K57 2017 (print) | LCC F592.7 (ebook) |
DDC 917.804/2--dc23
LC record available at https://lccn.loc.gov/2016054484

Editorial Director: David McNamara
Editor: Fletcher Doyle
Copy Editor: Nathan Heidelberger
Associate Art Director: Amy Greenan
Designer: Raul Rodriguez
Production Coordinator: Karol Szymczuk

CONTENTS

Expanding the Country

W hen people today look at a map of the United States of America, they see a huge country. But that wasn't always the case. Back in 1800, the country was about one-third as big as the **continental** United States is now. It stretched from the Atlantic Ocean in the east to the Mississippi River in the west, and from the Great Lakes in the north almost to the Gulf of Mexico in the south. This area was about 1,000 miles (1,609 kilometers) by 1,000 miles.

Where did most Americans live at this time? About two-thirds lived within 50 miles (80 km) of the Atlantic Ocean. Wilderness made up much of the young nation. The United States had timber, animals, and lots of other natural resources. Americans could explore and use these lands and resources to boost their own wealth and standard of living.

In March 1801, Thomas Jefferson was sworn in as the third president of the United States. According to the census of 1800, the country had 5,308,483 people. This was an increase in population of 1,379,269 people from the first US census in 1790. Many would say that the United States had plenty of room for all these people, but most people were not Thomas Jefferson. Besides being extremely intelligent, the

Rembrandt Peale painted this portrait of Thomas Jefferson in January 1805.

new president was also a dreamer. One of Jefferson's dreams involved expanding the territory of the United States. After all, many European nations like Great Britain had vast empires. These empires brought new foods, information, and other resources to their people.

Jefferson had visions of a country that stretched from the Atlantic to the Pacific Oceans. He believed that it was "the natural progress of things ... for [the] government to gain ground." This new-and-improved United States would be powerful. It would also be rich.

How could such a young country like the United States transform into the nation Jefferson dreamed of? One might guess that expanding the nation's territory would require conflict with those who controlled bordering territories. However, that was not the case. Through negotiations and skillful planning, the fledgling nation was able to double in

Population Growth During Westward Expansion

The first census of the United States was taken in 1790. A new census has been taken every ten years since that time. Below is the population of the United States as measured in each census during expansion, and the percentage the population increased since the previous census.

Year	Population	Percent Change
1790	3,929,214	–
1800	5,308,483	35.1
1810	7,239,881	36.4
1820	9,638,453	33.1
1830	12,860,702	33.4
1840	17,063,353	32.7
1850	23,191,876	35.9
1860	31,443,321	35.6
1870	38,558,371	22.6

size without war. The United States experienced a gigantic and rapid westward expansion through something known as the Louisiana Purchase. Many historians refer to this as the greatest real estate deal in history.

The United States bought the land now known as the Louisiana Purchase from France in 1803 for $15 million. This purchase added 828,000 square miles (2.1 million square kilometers) to the United States. This new territory stretched west from the Mississippi River to the Rocky Mountains. Parts of fifteen current US states were carved out of land that Jefferson purchased.

Lewis and Clark and Exploring
the Louisiana Purchase

President Jefferson arranged for an expedition to explore the lands of the Louisiana Purchase. Jefferson's secretary, Meriwether Lewis, and an army friend named William Clark led this exploration party. The team became known as the Corps of Discovery. These men brought back huge amounts of information about the lands and people of the Louisiana Territory—a tremendous gift to the new nation.

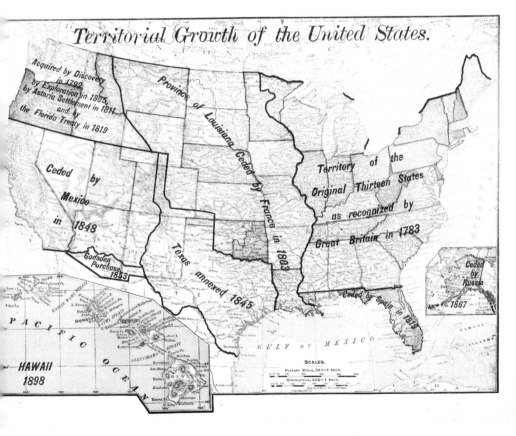

Printed in 1900, this map shows the steps by which the territory of United States grew over time. This map appeared in *Spofford's Atlas of the World*.

Artist Jacques-Louis David painted this portrait of Napoléon in 1805.

Growing the Nation

W hen Thomas Jefferson took office as president, the United States was still a very young nation. Elsewhere in North America, other nations claimed territory that is part of the present-day United States. Great Britain was one. Spain was another. In 1800, Spain claimed quite a bit of North American land, including the Louisiana Territory. Spain also ruled the two Floridas at that time. West Florida covered what are now the southern parts of Alabama and Mississippi, and eastern Louisiana. East Florida included most of what is now the state of Florida

Soon after taking office, Jefferson started hearing rumors. They were about an agreement between Spain and France. Jefferson heard that Spain had given the territories of Louisiana and New Orleans to France. Why did this matter? Unlike Spain, whose power at that time was declining, France was a strong nation. Napoléon Bonaparte was its leader.

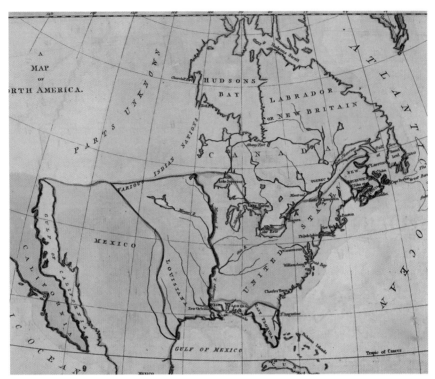

This 1803 map by John Luffman shows part of North America, including the United States, Louisiana, California, Mexico, Labrador and "Parts Unknown."

In 1802, American officials in France discovered that these rumors were true. France and Spain had signed a secret treaty called the Treaty of San Ildefonso. According to this treaty, Spain returned Louisiana to France—France had ceded the territory to Spain as part of a larger settlement to end the French and Indian War in 1763. In return, France gave Spain land in Italy, known as the Kingdom of Etruria.

Jefferson wondered what Napoléon's plans would be if he acquired so much land in North America. France's foreign minister, Charles-Maurice de Talleyrand, provided the answer. He wrote at the time of the treaty:

> Let the Court of Madrid cede these districts to France, and from that moment the power of

Lewis and Clark and Exploring the Louisiana Purchase

America is bounded by the limit which it may suit the interests and the tranquility of France and Spain to assign here. The French Republic ... will be the wall of brass forever impenetrable to the combined efforts of England and America.

Napoléon wanted to build a bigger and stronger empire. That would never do, in Jefferson's mind. He had his own plans for conquering the continent.

New Orleans

A very important part of the territory France acquired from Spain was New Orleans. As Thomas Jefferson stated, "There is on the globe one single spot, the possessor of which is our natural and habitual enemy. It is New Orleans, through which the produce of three-eighths of our territory must pass to market." This port city was essential to the trade of goods in the United States.

Back in the early 1800s, there weren't roads that connected the markets and cities of the US East Coast with the farmers

J. L. Bouqueto de Woiseri created this work to celebrate the Louisiana Purchase. The eagle's banner reads "Under My Wings Every Thing Prospers."

and people in the country's western territories. Today, a farmer in Kentucky can send his crops by truck to the East Coast in less than a day. In Jefferson's day, a farmer would have to send his goods by boat down the Mississippi River to New Orleans. They would continue by water to the Gulf of Mexico, around the tip of Florida, and north up the Atlantic coast to New York. It was a much slower process.

When Spain was in charge of New Orleans, it gave US citizens free access to the Mississippi River. It also allowed Americans the "right of deposit" there. This allowed the American people to use the river to ship their goods all the way through New Orleans without paying duties to Spanish authorities. If France changed this tax policy, it would be a huge problem for Americans. Merchants would have to charge more for their goods to cover the taxes. So would farmers and fur trappers.

President Jefferson decided to take action, just in case France decided to tax Americans for using the Mississippi and New Orleans. He sent a **diplomat** named Robert Livingston to Paris. Livingston had helped draft the Declaration of Independence decades earlier. Jefferson told Livingston to buy New Orleans from France. Livingston worked hard to convince the French to sell these lands to the United States. He used his best negotiating skills but had no luck.

Jefferson knew that France might not sell the desired lands to the United States. However, he had hoped they would at least agree to give Americans free passage down the Mississippi River and trading rights in New Orleans's port. In October of 1802, Americans lost their right to store their goods in the warehouses of New Orleans.

People in the United States, particularly those living in the western territories, were furious. Some talked of war. Senator James Ross of Pennsylvania, a member of the opposition **Federalist** Party, publicly supported taking possession of the city of New Orleans with fifty thousand men.

Lewis and Clark and Exploring
the Louisiana Purchase

Making Deals in Paris

President Jefferson and his secretary of state, James Madison, wanted to resolve the issue in New Orleans. They believed in using diplomatic channels (talking things through) to do this. As the situation at home grew worse, Thomas Jefferson made a recommendation. He proposed that James Monroe travel to Paris to help Livingston with the negotiations. Monroe had been the US minister to France under George Washington. Also, Monroe owned land in Kentucky. He was an advocate for the people in the western territories.

Jefferson gave Monroe instructions to spend up to $10 million to buy New Orleans and part or all of East and West Florida (these lands still belonged to Spain, however, and wouldn't become part of the United States until 1819). If this bid didn't work out, Monroe was told to try to buy only New Orleans. The last option was to secure US access to the port and the Mississippi River. President Jefferson said, "All eyes, all hopes, are now fixed on you … for on the event of this mission depends the future destinies of this republic."

While Monroe was traveling by sea to France, Napoléon was meeting with his finance minister, François de Barbé-Marbois, about France's money problems. France was having conflicts with people in Europe and the Caribbean. After the discussions between Napoléon and Barbé-Marbois, France changed its policy on selling land to the United States.

On April 11, 1803 (the day before James Monroe arrived in Paris), Talleyrand made Livingston an amazing offer. France would sell all of Louisiana, including New Orleans, to the United States. But France was asking for more money than President Jefferson had given them permission to spend.

What could Livingston and Monroe do? It would have taken too long to get permission from President Jefferson for the increased spending through letters traveling by sea. So the two men negotiated for the best deal they could. On

Why Napoléon Sold Louisiana

The Louisiana Territory was huge. It had rivers, forests, and many natural resources. It also included the valuable port city of New Orleans. One might wonder why France suddenly changed its mind and agreed to sell all of Louisiana to the United States. The answer involves world affairs.

Napoléon was a brilliant military leader who had conquered large areas of Europe. At one point, Napoléon hoped to create his own powerful base in the Americas. But France was having trouble with its Caribbean colony Saint-Domingue, which is now called Haïti. The colony's sugar plantations made lots of money for France. But slaves and free blacks were rebelling against French rule. Toussaint L'Ouverture, the leader of the Haitian independence movement, had built an army to fight the French. These rebels started winning battles against the French army.

In 1801, Napoléon sent tens of thousands of men to Saint-Domingue. In addition to L'Ouverture's forces, malaria and yellow fever killed many French fighters. The French captured L'Ouverture and put him in jail. Napoleon even sent another wave of French forces from the Louisiana Territory to Saint-Domingue. However, the French lost control of the colony.

Sending soldiers from France to the Caribbean was expensive. So was maintaining an empire from thousands of miles away. François de Barbé-Marbois, Napoléon's finance minister, advised him to let go of his dream of an empire in America. It looked like France might end up with a war against Britain. Britain and France were fighting over control of Europe, and Europe was more important to Napoléon than America. France would need cash for its war chest. Selling Louisiana would provide money to France.

Another advantage to France was that if the United States controlled these lands, Britain could not spread its influence further over the New World.

This hand-colored woodcut depicts Toussaint L'Ouverture, known as the liberator of Haiti.

April 30, France and the United States reached an agreement. The United States would pay $15 million for the Louisiana Territory, including New Orleans.

This image shows James Monroe and Robert Livingston negotiating with Talleyrand for the Louisiana Purchase in April 1803.

Months later, the news of Livington's and Monroe's success finally reached Washington, DC. On June 30, 1803, the *Boston Independent Chronicle* was the first newspaper to announce the news about Louisiana. Its headline read "Louisiana Ceded to the United States!"

Was the Louisiana Purchase a done deal? Not quite. The Senate had to **ratify** the Louisiana Purchase Treaty. The House of Representatives had to fund it. Finally, the President needed to sign it.

Constitutional Challenge

Thomas Jefferson recognized that adding these new lands was a tremendous opportunity for the United States. He thought that western expansion was the solution to the nation's health. In his view, land ownership—especially that of small farms—was an important part of independence and **virtue**.

If the United States wanted to provide enough land as the population grew, it would need to continue expanding.

Jefferson also had some concerns. He wasn't sure if such a land purchase was allowed by the US Constitution. Jefferson had always believed that the powers of the federal government should be strictly interpreted. Article IV, Section 3 of the US Constitution says:

> New States may be admitted by the Congress into this Union; but no new States shall be formed or erected within the Jurisdiction of any other State; nor any State be formed by the Junction of two or more States, or parts of States, without the Consent of the Legislatures of the States concerned as well as of the Congress.

The Constitution said that new states could be added to the country. It didn't say anything about adding foreign territories. Jefferson thought it was necessary to add a constitutional amendment to address this issue. In 1803, he wrote in a letter to former Delaware governor and informal advisor John Dickinson:

> The General Government had no powers but such as the Constitution gives it … It has not given it power of holding foreign territory, and still less of incorporating it into the Union. An amendment of the Constitution seems necessary for this.

President Jefferson drafted an amendment that would give permission for the purchase of Louisiana **retroactively**. However, Jefferson's cabinet members told him an amendment was a bad idea. Senator Wilson Cary Nicholas of Virginia worried that mentioning an amendment might cause some of the Old Republicans to refuse to approve

The PRAIRIE DOG sickened at the sting of the HORNET — or a Diplomatic Puppet exhibiting his Deceptions!

James Akin's 1804 political cartoon depicts Jefferson as a prairie dog being stung by a hornet (with Napoléon's head) and coughing up millions.

the treaty. Old Republicans opposed any alterations to the US Constitution.

Thomas Jefferson was hardly the only American to have serious concerns about the Louisiana Purchase. While his concerns largely focused on the constitutionality of the treaty, many people had spoken against the idea of westward expansion for more than a decade. Paine Wingate, a Federalist senator from Massachusetts, expressed his concerns in a letter to New Hampshire businessman and civic leader Samuel Lane dated June 2, 1788:

> It is true that the [West] is immensely large, is an excellent soil, and capable of supporting a vast number of inhabitants, but I think they will draw off our most valuable and enterprising young men and will impede the population of our old States and prevent establishment of manufactures. Upon the whole, I doubt whether,

Lewis and Clark and Exploring the Louisiana Purchase

Two-Party System

George Washington, the first president of the United States, opposed political factions, but the first two political parties formed during his tenure.

The Federalists, who counted John Adams and Alexander Hamilton among their members, favored a strong central government. Its members wrote the Federalist Papers. Among the contributions the Federalists made to the country before dissolving in 1820 are a national judicial system, a national economy, and principles of foreign policy.

The Federalists were opposed by the Democratic-Republican Party. It emphasized states' rights, pushed for the Bill of Rights, and backed a strict interpretation of the Constitution to limit the power of the federal government. Thomas Jefferson founded this party. It favored an agrarian-based economy and a democratic, decentralized government.

in our day, that country will not be a damage to us rather than an advantage.

Many Federalists also worried that agreeing to the Louisiana Purchase would reduce their political power. They worried that voters in the new western states would side with Jefferson and his Democratic-Republican Party on national political matters. Many thought that these new states would reduce the Federalist majority in some regions and maybe even lead to the extinction of their political party. All but one Federalist senator voted against the ratification of the Louisiana Purchase Treaty.

High Costs and Bad Lands

Some Americans were concerned about the high price of buying Louisiana. Former congressman Fisher Ames reflected the sentiment of these people, stating, "We are to give money of which we have too little for land of which we already have too much." The *Columbian Centinel*, a Boston newspaper, had this to say on the matter: "THE ADDITION OF LOUISIANA IS ONLY A PRETENSE FOR DRAWING AN IMMENSE SUM OF MONEY FROM US." The *Hartford Courant* shared the Federalists' worries in print with its readers:

> Fifteen million dollars for bogs, mountains, and Indians! Fifteen million dollars for uninhabited wasteland and refuge for criminals! And for what purposes? To enhance the power of Virginia's politicians. To pour millions into the coffers of Napoléon on the eve of war with England.

Many Americans feared that the United States could not act independently if it owed lots of money to other countries. The United States had to borrow millions of dollars from European banks to buy Louisiana, which it would have to pay back with interest. Some Americans wanted foreign nations out of their continent—financially and in person.

Another argument against buying the Louisiana Territory from France was that the United States didn't need more land. People believed that the young nation was plenty big and already had room for people to spread out and settle.

Slavery and the Louisiana Purchase

A large debate over western expansion and the Louisiana Purchase centered upon the question of whether this vast new territory would allow slavery. The South was in favor of

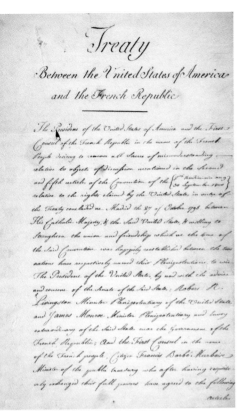

This original document is the treaty which ceded France's Louisiana Territory to the United States.

the expansion of slavery into the new lands. The North was very much against such an expansion.

Senator Timothy Pickering of Massachusetts thought the purchase was an attempt to expand Southern slaveholders' power. And Uriah Tracy, a senator from Connecticut said, "The relative strength which this admission gives the southern and western interest is contradictory to the principles of our original union." Those opposed to slavery in the new lands worried that it would be tough for non-slaveholding white settlers to compete with slaveholders. It would be cheaper for the slaveholders to grow and sell crops since they had unpaid laborers.

Some people in the South were opposed to western expansion. They feared that the new states created in the West would vote against slavery and tip the nation's balance in favor of Free States (as opposed to slave states). Congress met in October 1803 to consider the Louisiana Purchase with a pending deadline. According to the terms of Monroe's and Livingston's negotiations, the United States only had six months from the April 30 agreement to get the treaty approved. After two days of debate, the Senate ratified the Louisiana Purchase Treaty on October 20, 1803. The United States formally took possession of this land on December 30, 1803.

CHAPTER TWO

Conquering Challenges

Long before the United States actually acquired the Louisiana Territory, Thomas Jefferson had plans for the area. He wanted explorers to find out what lay beyond the borders of the United States. President Jefferson asked Congress, in a letter sent in January 1803, for $2,500 to fund an expedition to explore the West. He characterized it as a commercial exploration and not a move toward expansion to avoid opposition from the Federalists. Congress approved his request by a large margin during the winter of 1803.

That spring, President Jefferson selected Meriwether Lewis, his private secretary, to lead the expedition. A former army officer, Lewis was an **amateur** scientist and a skilled frontiersman. Lewis was allowed to choose a co-leader for the expedition. He invited his dear friend William Clark. Clark had spent much of his life on the Kentucky and Ohio frontiers. There he had learned how to negotiate with Native Americans and how to fight. Clark accepted Lewis's invitation.

Passport Problems

Back in the early 1800s, people didn't go to an office to get a passport for travel. Letters had to be written to those in power in the lands where one wanted to travel. Thomas Jefferson wrote these letters for Lewis. He wanted this expedition to be able to travel freely in foreign territory. At the time, Britain claimed ownership of the Oregon Territory. Also, much of the Southwest was considered part of the Spanish Empire.

William Clark as painted circa 1807.

In his letters to these European nations, Jefferson described the expedition as a scientific mission instead of a "commercial" trip. Britain, France, and Spain would have been opposed to the idea that the United States was trying to look for business opportunities and trading partners in their territories.

France and England issued passports, but Spain never did. Why? The Spanish ambassador doubted Jefferson's stated **motives** for the expedition.

Getting Ready

Much of 1803 was spent preparing for the expedition. Lewis went to Philadelphia to learn about **zoology**, **botany**, and mineralogy. He studied how to navigate using the stars. Lewis also learned about medicine from the highly regarded Dr. Benjamin Rush.

American physician and educator Benjamin Rush at his desk

Clark bought supplies for the expedition. There were woolen blankets, tents, scientific instruments, rifles, powder horns (to hold gunpowder), and lead (to make bullets). The expedition needed weapons for hunting, but they were also for protection. Lewis and Clark were not entirely sure how the Native American groups living west of American soil would receive them. Some groups were known to be hostile toward strangers.

Lewis and Clark would cross the homelands of many tribes. They purchased a variety of gifts for the Native Americans—colorful beads, knives, mirrors, tobacco, and whiskey. They also brought at least eighty-nine peace medals as gifts. These had a picture of President Thomas Jefferson on one side and people shaking hands on the other. On the backside of the medals were written the words "Peace" and "Friendship."

When the Lewis and Clark expedition departed on their journey in May 1804, their party consisted of more than thirty men. Collectively this group was known as the Corps of Discovery. The men were handpicked

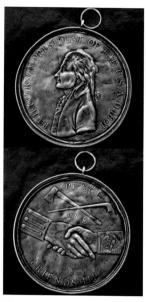

These are peace medals carried by the expedition.

for particular skills. For example, Patrick Gass was a carpenter. Silas Goodrich was a skilled fisherman. Some of the men had white fathers and Native American mothers.

A Message from the President

As Lewis and Clark traveled along the Missouri River, they encountered many Native American tribes. By the time the Corps of Discovery made its way to the northern plains, there had already been more than a half-century of contact between Native groups and white travelers.

President Jefferson had given Lewis and Clark clear instructions about the messages he wanted conveyed to the Native Americans. The captains were to explain to the tribal leaders that their lands belonged now to the United States. They also needed to inform the Native peoples that President Thomas Jefferson was to be considered their "great father." Here is an example of the language that Captain Meriwether Lewis used in his speech to the Yankton Sioux on August 30, 1804:

> Children. Your old fathers, the French and the Spaniards, have gone beyond the great lake toward the rising sun … Children. The great chief of the seventeen great nations of America has become your only father. He has commanded us … to undertake this long journey … Children. Do these things which your great father advises and be happy … lest by one false step you should bring down upon your nation the displeasure of your great father … Follow these counsels and you will have nothing to fear … and future ages will make you outnumber the trees in the forest.

Giving such a speech to the independent and proud Native Americans was a bold move. Many would say this behavior was offensive. After all, Native American tribes had been living on the land for many thousands of years before the Corps of Discovery ever set foot in these territories.

Native Americans did not expect nor welcome politics and **diplomacy.** They often accepted the gifts that the explorers brought them out of curiosity, politeness, or hospitality. But the Native Americans did not believe that these objects took away from their own national **sovereignty.** They didn't think some token gifts suddenly bound them to a great father who was far away. They were disturbed by the idea that this expedition party was telling them to be obedient to the wishes of a leader in Washington, DC.

Trouble with the Sioux

In the summer of 1804, the expedition reached the homelands of the Missouri and Oto nations in what is now the border of Iowa and Nebraska. These groups, which hunted bison and farmed, were friendly overall. However, Lewis wanted the Otos and Missouris to stop raiding the other tribes in the area. These Native peoples were disappointed by the gifts of tobacco, beads, and paint. Having seen the huge supply of materials on the expedition's keelboat, they felt their gifts were rather small. The Otos and Missouris were looking for an open-trade system that was more reliable. Lewis and Clark could not guarantee such a system at that time, so not much was accomplished in this initial **council.**

The outcome of the interactions between the Missouri and Oto peoples was acceptable, but not terrific. However, once Lewis and Clark entered Sioux territory, things changed for the worse. The Teton branch of the Sioux (also known as the Lakotas) were known for being warlike. They attacked the **sedentary** tribes in the region. Their reputation had reached Washington, even before the expedition left. They had intimidated both the Spanish and the French, and controlled trade along the Missouri River.

Lewis and Clark and Exploring
the Louisiana Purchase

Lewis and Clark hold a council with the Omaha and Oto tribes at Council Bluffs, Iowa. This image comes from Patrick Gass's journal.

The Corps of Discovery encountered the Teton Sioux near modern-day Pierre, South Dakota. Clark had written that it was essential for the expedition to treat this group "in the most friendly and **conciliatory** manner." Clark was nervous when Chief Buffalo Medicine and some of the other chiefs came to talk with the expedition. They presented him (as the leading chief) with a red military coat, a cocked hat, and a peace medal. The chiefs thought the corps' gifts were not adequate. They wanted more **tribute**. They thought a **pirogue** (boat) laden with gifts was appropriate.

Three warriors seized the bow cable of the boat. They aimed their arrows at the expedition party. Clark drew his sword. His fellow party members loaded the cannon. Chief Black Buffalo intervened. He took the cable and ordered the warriors away from the boat.

Despite this hostility, the Corps of Discovery remained with the Teton Sioux for three days. They tried to build bridges through ceremonies and festivities. But when the expedition went to move on along their journey, there was more trouble. Again the Sioux wanted more from the expedition. They demanded that the expedition remain with them. Eventually Chief Black Buffalo convinced the other Sioux chiefs to let the expedition pass.

The Mandan and the Blackfeet

After fleeing from their troubles with the Sioux, Lewis and Clark's party headed north into present-day North Dakota. Winter was nearly upon them. The Mandan people let the Corps of Discovery build a fort and spend the winter on their land.

The expedition didn't have the dramatic conflicts in the Mandan village that they'd had with the Sioux. However, the explorers' behavior confused the Mandans (and many other Native American groups). Most white settlers who interacted

This woodcut shows members of the Corps of Discovery building Fort Mandan.

Lewis and Clark and Exploring
the Louisiana Purchase

with Native Americans came as trading partners. Lewis and Clark talked with these Native peoples about trade, but the expedition had a clear agenda. They were trying to convince the Native Americans to shift their trade away from the Canadians. Lewis's party wanted the tribes to focus on trading with the American commercial system based in St. Louis, Missouri. The Mandan people found the Americans stingy when bargaining.

Probably the worst conflict the expedition had with the Native Americans involved the Blackfeet tribe. In July 1806, Lewis was with a small band of men from the Corps of Discovery in present-day Montana. Clark had gone south with some men to explore the Yellowstone River.

Lewis and his men met a small group of young Blackfeet men near the Two Medicine River. Lewis gave the leader a peace medal and a small flag. The groups decided to camp together for the night. Lewis mentioned, using sign language, that the Americans were now allies of the Shoshone and Nez Percé tribes—traditionally both enemies of the Blackfeet. Lewis said these other tribes would receive supplies and guns from the United States. This plan of arming their enemies seemed a direct threat to the Blackfeet men. Giving guns to their enemies would weaken the Blackfeet tribe's power.

The next morning, the young Blackfeet grabbed some of the expedition's guns and tried to escape. Private Reuben Field stabbed one thief in the heart. Lewis shot another man dead. Lewis later wrote:

> I called to them … that I would shoot them if they did not give me my horse and raised my gun, one of them jumped behind a rock and spoke to the other who turned around and [stopped] at the distance of 30 steps from me and I shot him through the belly, he fell to his knees and on his [right] elbow from which

Published in 1811, Patrick Gass's illustration shows the fight with the Blackfeet.

position he partly raised himself up and fired at me, and turning himself about crawled in behind a rock which was a few feet from him.

Lewis and his men fled from the scene. They were worried what the Blackfeet would do if they ever caught up with them. Lewis and his men did manage to escape. However, Blackfeet war parties later killed three former Corps of Discovery members.

Spain Tries to Intercept Corps

Native Americans weren't the only people to have issues with the Lewis and Clark expedition. Both the British and the Spanish were not happy about the Americans' mission. The British saw the expedition as competition in the fur trade. It also threatened the alliances the British had already made with the Native Americans in the region. To protect its own

Lewis and Clark and Exploring the Louisiana Purchase

interests, Great Britain sought to increase its presence in the Pacific Northwest. American claims to this area had been contested in the past.

The Spanish government tried to **intercept** the Lewis and Clark expedition. Why? The Spanish believed any American expedition traveling into the Louisiana Territory would likely lead to the United States trying to conquer Spanish territories to the south and west. The borders of the territory Jefferson bought were not completely clear, according to the terms of the Louisiana Purchase Treaty, so Spain was right to suspect that the Corps of Discovery might intrude into Spanish territory.

Spain was also afraid to let the expedition get into contact with the Native Americans on the southern plains. New trading partners like the Americans might have different goods to buy and sell, better prices, or other opportunities for the Native Americans. Spanish leaders worried that the Lewis and Clark expedition might try to turn the Native Americans they met against the Spanish.

The first two parties sent by the Spanish to block Lewis and Clark didn't come into contact with the Corps of Discovery. Instead, they just wandered around modern-day Nebraska and Kansas. This isn't terribly surprising. After all, the Missouri River was far from the Spanish home base, and the areas these parties were traveling through were vast.

The third party bumped into a group led by Zebulon Pike, which had been sent by Jefferson to explore the West.

While both Europeans and Native Americans opposed the Lewis and Clark expedition, these conflicts did not stop the Corps of Discovery from succeeding in its many goals.

CHAPTER THREE

Meeting Goals

The expedition of Meriwether Lewis, William Clark, and the Corps of Discovery lasted from May 1804 to late September 1806. The bold and brave team traveled more than 7,689 miles (12,374 km) from Camp DuBois near St. Louis, Missouri, to the Pacific Ocean in Oregon and back to Missouri.

President Thomas Jefferson had given Lewis and Clark many goals for their expedition. One was to learn about the natural features of the newly acquired lands west of the Mississippi River. This was an especially huge task, given how much area there was to cover. In this regard, the Corps of Discovery was highly successful. One example of their success is that Lewis and Clark's team greatly added to the knowledge of the continent's volcanoes. The first volcano they spotted was Mount Hood in present-day Oregon. They also observed layers of lava flows at the Columbia Plateau in the Pacific Northwest.

Lewis and Clark and Exploring
the Louisiana Purchase

Harry Weber created this bronze sculpture titled *The Captain's Return* to celebrate the bicentennial of Lewis and Clark's return to St. Louis, Missouri.

Among Jefferson's goals for the expedition was finding a water passage across the continent—what was called the Northwest Passage. He wrote in his letter to Lewis:

> The object of your mission is to explore the Missouri River, and such principal stream of it, as, by its course and communications with the waters of the Pacific Ocean may offer the most

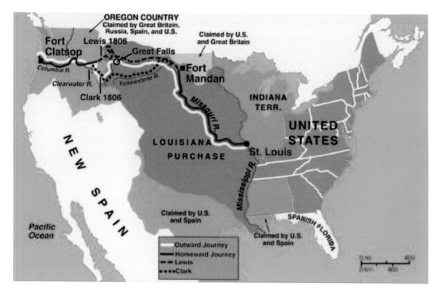

This map shows the route of the Lewis and Clark expedition. Yellow shows the outward journey and red is the return trip.

> direct and practicable water communication
> across this continent … Those who come after
> us will … fill up the canvas we begin.

Jefferson, like explorers through the centuries, had dreamed of a simple water route across North America. Such a route would be faster than existing land or waterways for getting goods to markets in Asia and from the West to the more populated eastern United States. Jefferson imagined people would more quickly settle the West if they traveled on the Northwest Passage.

Using scientific measurements and observations, the explorers made accurate reports on the course, depth, and current of the Missouri River. They mapped its **tributaries.** They discovered that neither the Missouri nor the Columbia Rivers could be navigated (by water) all the way to their source. There was no such thing as the Northwest Passage. It took lots of hard labor, such as carrying boats around waterfalls and over rough terrain, to make this discovery. And

Lewis and Clark and Exploring
the Louisiana Purchase

while it was disappointing on many levels, this knowledge meant that another goal had been met. Lewis and Clark recorded facts about the geography of their young nation and shared this knowledge with the American people.

Making Maps

William Clark was the main mapmaker for the Corps of Discovery. He'd learned mapmaking during his time in the army in the 1790s. During the expedition, Clark prepared four kinds of maps. He sketched small, page-sized maps in his journals. Sometimes these small maps were very detailed. Some showed features that impacted travelers' ability to navigate rivers, like rapids, narrows, and falls.

An excellent example of a journal map is the one Clark created of the Great Falls of the Columbia River in the Pacific Northwest. He used arrows to show the direction of the river currents. He used different colors—yellow for sand and brown for rock formations. He drew in places for canoe portages around the falls. And there are also notes about where various Native American nations lived on the map.

Both Lewis and Clark copied or drew maps based on information they'd gotten from Native Americans and traders. From St. Louis to the Great Falls of the mighty Missouri River, a French boatman who had already been to the region helped to guide the expedition. He and other traders provided information for the maps created during this beginning of their trip. As the Corps of Discovery traveled farther west, the party relied more on Native American maps for knowledge of the landscape beyond what they could see. Sometimes these maps were sketched on the ground. Other times they were drawn on animal skin. Lewis and Clark copied these maps onto map paper or into their journals.

During the winter of 1804, a Mandan chief named Big White (or Shahaka) gave lots of information to Clark about the Yellowstone River area of Wyoming. The chief had just

Doug Hyde's *Hospitality of the Nez Perce* sculpture shows Chief Twisted Hair sharing his knowledge of the land with Lewis and Clark.

been on a hunting trip there. Clark used this knowledge to create the first map of the Yellowstone River and its tributaries.

Most of the Native American maps which Lewis and Clark collected feature areas west of the Rocky Mountains. Chief Twisted Hair of the Nez Percé tribe drew a map that showed the rivers that lay beyond his camp. On October 18, 1805, William Clark wrote in his journal about another Native American map:

> The Great Chief and one of the Chim-nâ pum nation drew me a Sketch of the Columbia

[River] above and the tribes of his nation,
living on the bank, and its waters, and the Tâpe
têtt river which falls in 18 miles above on the
westerly side.

Clark made composite maps of the West, combining information from various maps into one larger map. But the most common maps Clark made are called compass traverse maps. These showed the route that the expedition traveled each day. It took many scientific instruments and lots of time to create these detailed maps. They are some of the most important sources of information to come from the Lewis and Clark expedition. Knowledge of the continent's rivers, plains, mountains, and other landforms was greatly expanded thanks to Clark's and the Corps' efforts.

Journals and Scientific Exploration

President Jefferson was very clear in his demands for Lewis and Clark to keep detailed journals. The men were supposed to record everything they saw and experienced. Most of the other expedition members also kept journals.

The men wrote about the conditions of the rivers as they traveled. They noted the plants and animals they encountered at every step of the journey. The team jotted down information about the food they ate and health troubles they had. And, of course, the men wrote about the people they met from Missouri to Oregon. No topic was off limits. In the days before cameras, journals provided snapshots into life on the trail.

Throughout their travels, Lewis and Clark's team acted as scientists. They observed their surroundings and conducted experiments. For example, they measured the speed and distance traveled on the water each day. They did this using "log line reels." A log line is made of a rope divided into known lengths. The line would be attached to a stationary

Women Help the Expedition

When Lewis and Clark headed out from Missouri in 1804, their expedition party was all men. In November 1804, the Corps of Discovery met a Native American woman named Sacagawea and her French Canadian husband, Toussaint Charbonneau. Sacagawea belonged to the Shoshone tribe. She spoke Shoshone and Hidatsa, her husband spoke Hidatsa and French, and corps member Francois Labiche spoke French and English. Therefore Sacagawea could speak to Lewis or Clark only through two other men.

Sacagawea was hired by the expedition as a guide and translator. Shortly after she joined the expedition, she gave birth to her son, Jean Baptiste. When the corps needed horses to cross the Bitterroot Mountains, she negotiated on the expedition's behalf. There were many times on the journey that Sacagawea's presence helped the party. Why? Native Americans knew if a woman with her child was with a group that it was not a war party. Sacagawea was brave and worked hard. She gathered edible plants, picked berries, and dug roots for the team to eat. When the boat she was on nearly capsized, Sacagawea recovered many of the precious items (papers and supplies) that were nearly lost.

There were other Native women who helped the Corps of Discovery, but Lewis and Clark only identify two by name in their journals. Besides Sacagawea, the second was Watkuweis. The expedition party had just spent a grueling week and a half getting through the Bitterroot Mountains. The men were weak and hungry when the Nez Percé tribe found them. The tribal leaders debated how to treat these strangers with guns. Watkuweis came to

Artist Alfred Russell created this painting titled *Sacajawea Guiding the Lewis and Clark Expedition* in 1904.

the corps' rescue. As a young girl, she had been captured by the Blackfeet. During this time, she came to know some white fur traders. These strangers were kind to her. Watkuweis urged her tribe not to harm Lewis and Clark's party. Thanks to her efforts, the Nez Percés provided guides, horses, food, and directions to the party both in the fall of 1805 and the spring of 1806.

object or buoy near the boat in the water. When the boat moved forward, the men could time how long it took for the line to be stretched out. The men used log lines to determine how fast the current was. They made "course and distance" tables each day to keep track of the direction and distance for every segment of the trip. The corps also tried to record the weather patterns of the West.

President Jefferson wanted information about the plants and animals of the Louisiana Territory and beyond. The Corps of Discovery took detailed notes on the appearances and behaviors of all kinds of living creatures and plant life. For example, the corps spent the winter of 1805 to 1806 in Oregon. On February 26, Lewis wrote all about a fish called the eulachon, or candlefish, in his journal. He also made a life-size sketch of the fish, which was a food source for the Native population. He described where it was found and gave many details about its appearance. He noted that the fish was so oily that after it had been dried it would burn like a candle.

William Clark's detailed sketch comes from the journal he kept during the expedition.

Collecting Specimens

Over the course of the expedition, Lewis and Clark's party saw grizzly bears, coyotes, antelopes, and many other animals they had never seen before. They recorded observations of 122 animals and 178 plants that were not previously known to the American people. This was a huge increase in the scientific knowledge of our nation.

Lewis and Clark and Exploring
the Louisiana Purchase

The Corps of Discovery didn't just write about plants and animals. They also collected specimens. Meriwether Lewis sent a magpie, a black and white bird, back to Washington for President Jefferson to see for himself.

One of the most entertaining stories about specimen collection involves prairie dogs. Lewis and Clark came across their first prairie dog "town" in September 1804 near modern-day Fort Randall Dam, Nebraska. William Clark wrote in his journal on September 7 about the expedition's interactions with these animals:

> Discovered a Village of Small animals that burrow in the [ground] (those animals are Called by the french Petite Chien) Killed one and Caught one [alive] by [pouring] a great quantity of Water in his hole we attempted to dig to the beds of one of those animals, after digging 6 feet [1.8 meters], found by running a pole down that we were not half way to his Lodge ... The Village of those animals [covered] about 4 acres [1.6 hectares] of Ground on a gradual [descent] of a hill and Contains great numbers of holes on the top of which those little animals Set erect, make a [whistling] noise and [when alarmed] Step into their hole. we [poured] into one of those holes 5 barrels of Water without filling it. Those Animals are about the Size of a Small [squirrel] ... except the ears which is Shorter, his tail like a ground [squirrel] which they shake & whistle when [alarmed]. the toe nails long, they have fine fur.

The expedition included a live prairie dog among the plant, animal, and rock samples sent to President Jefferson from Fort Mandan, North Dakota, in 1805. This shipment arrived at Monticello on August 25, 1805.

Observing the Native Americans

Another major goal of the Lewis and Clark expedition was for the party to observe and make contact with the Native Americans of the West. President Jefferson wanted to know what they did for a living. What did they eat, and how did they prepare their foods? What were the relations between Native American men and women like? Jefferson wanted the Corps of Discovery to study Native American languages and customs. He wanted to learn more about their medical practices.

Every time that the Corps of Discovery encountered a Native American tribe, the men wrote down their observations. Sometimes these encounters lasted only a few days. Other times the expedition party spent longer in one place. For example, the expedition's members stayed in close proximity to the Mandans throughout the winter of 1804 through 1805.

No matter which tribe they were interacting with, Lewis, Clark, and many of the other officers took detailed notes. Sometimes their journals addressed hunting and farming techniques. The explorers described tribal homes, such as the earth lodges of the Plains Indians.

The explorers learned a lot from the Native peoples about traditional medicine. Even though Lewis and Clark did not always agree with the Native Americans' explanations of why illness happened, they often used Native remedies instead of their own. When Lewis was ill in June 1805, he drank two doses of liquid made with boiled chokecherry twigs. Just hours after taking this remedy, he felt totally well again.

Native Americans used the plains coneflower to cure a rattlesnake bite. The Cheyennes made a tea to relieve coughing from a plant now known as elephant's head (*Pedicularis groenlandica*). In the aftermath of the expedition, many Americans who were skeptical of professional medicine chose to use the Native cures that Clark had written down.

Lewis and Clark and Exploring
the Louisiana Purchase

York

Sacagawea is rightly celebrated as a vital member of the Corps of Discovery. Many Native Americans helped make the Lewis and Clark expedition a tremendous success. Another critical member of the Corps of Discovery was an African American man. William Clark brought his slave York with him on the expedition. York was about the same age as Clark.

York participated in all kinds of work. One journal entry written about York tells of him swimming to a sandbar to gather greens for the men's dinner. York also tended to Sergeant Charles Floyd when he was ill in August 1804. And while slaves weren't allowed to handle firearms unless 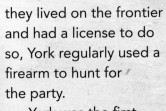 they lived on the frontier and had a license to do so, York regularly used a firearm to hunt for the party.

York was the first black man to cross North America north of Mexico. His strength and unique physical features fascinated many of the Native American peoples throughout the journey. Some historians have said that York's presence added to the prestige of the group in the eyes of the Native Americans.

The Mandans and other tribes were intrigued by York (*right*), William Clark's slave.

The corps' members learned how the tribes made canoes. Lewis sketched a Native American canoe in his journal. The team wrote about the ceremonies and dances they observed. Even beauty rituals were noted. For example, Lewis wrote in his journal about how the Chinook tribe flattened the heads of their female children (and some males as well).

In addition to learning about Native Americans, President Jefferson also instructed Lewis and Clark to recruit tribespeople to visit Washington and the eastern states. The president hoped that the Native peoples would be impressed with how civilized the United States was. Perhaps such travels would make the Native Americans want to trade with the country. Jefferson wanted to awe the Native Americans with how many people lived in the East. In a speech given to the Yankton Sioux in August 1804, Captain Lewis told the Native Americans:

> Children!—Know that the great chief who has thus offered you the hand of unalterable friendship, is the Great Chief of the Seventeen Great Nations of America, whose Cities are a[s] numerous as the Stars of the heavens, and whose people, like the grass of the Plains, cover with their cultivated fields and Wigwams, the wide extended country reaching from the western border of the Mississippi to the Great Lakes of the East, where the land ends and the Sun rises from the face of the Great Waters.

Another example of the success of the Lewis and Clark expedition is that a **delegation** of Native Americans did go to Washington. In March 1805, one Missouri chief and the leading Oto chief, Little Thief, were among those who met with President Jefferson. At this meeting, the US president said that he hoped for peace and promised goods in trade.

Lewis and Clark and Exploring the Louisiana Purchase

CHAPTER FOUR

From Sea to Shining Sea

Both the Louisiana Purchase and the Lewis and Clark expedition had lasting effects on the future of the United States. If these events had not happened, who knows how long the westward expansion of the country would have taken? Both events were essential for opening the North American continent to settlement by white Americans.

Before the Louisiana Purchase took place, there had been many arguments about whether it was a good idea. In hindsight, however, there is no question that it was an incredible bargain. For just pennies per acre, the lands of the Louisiana Purchase eventually became part of fifteen different American states. Some historians have said that along with the Declaration of Independence and the Constitution, the Louisiana Purchase is "one of the three things that created the modern United States."

Without this purchase, it's unlikely that the United States would have become the continental power it is today. The

A stockade is just one part of the recreation of Fort Clatsop on display at the Lewis and Clark National Historical Park in Oregon.

American ideas of freedom and democracy spread across the continent, thanks to this land acquisition. Jefferson wanted to establish "an empire for liberty," and for the non-Native settlers he succeeded.

The Louisiana Purchase also caused the international influence of the United States to grow by leaps and bounds. The Louisiana Purchase included nearly 830,000 square miles (2.15 million sq km) of territory. The territory was larger than Spain, France, Italy, Germany, Switzerland, the Netherlands, and the British Isles combined! It was also larger than the 1867 purchase of Alaska from Russia. That territory encompassed 586,412 square miles (1.5 million sq km) and cost $7.2 million. It was also ridiculed in Congress, which called it "Seward's Folly" after Secretary of State James H. Seward before ratifying the purchase by one vote.

The Louisiana Purchase added to the United States's wealth. At the time of the purchase, Thomas Jefferson didn't know the value of the natural resources within its boundaries. But even before Jefferson knew almost anything about this new territory, he was confident that this purchase would benefit the United States financially. He said, "The fertility of the country, its climate and extent, promise in due season important aids to our treasury, an ample provision for our posterity, and a wide-spread field for the blessings of

Lewis and Clark and Exploring
the Louisiana Purchase

freedom." What did Jefferson mean? He saw the Louisiana Purchase as an investment in the country's future. What an investment it turned out to be!

Gold, silver, and other ores from these lands have brought great opportunities to Americans. So have the vast forests and excellent grazing and farming lands.

Of course, the actual purchase of the Louisiana Territory was essential to the United States' westward expansion. Knowledge of this land was also important in getting people to move west. In this regard, Lewis and Clark were critical forces kick-starting the country's westward expansion.

The Oregon Trail

Lewis and Clark's expedition certainly paved the way for future Americans to travel and settle out west. Many areas that the Corps of Discovery traveled through became part of the Oregon Trail. The Oregon Trail was the main overland migration route used by people moving west. It was an essential piece of America's westward expansion. These travelers journeyed by foot, on horseback, and in wagons. It often took

Albert Bierstadt's 1863 work *Oregon Trail (Campfire)* shows life on the trail.

four to six months to make the trek. The Oregon Trail was mainly used between 1841 and 1869. Its importance declined once the transcontinental railroad was completed in 1869.

Later in the 1800s, the Lewis and Clark expedition was cited as an example of manifest destiny. What does that term mean? It was the belief or attitude that the United States not only could, but was destined to, stretch from one coast to the other. By bringing the American flag all the way across the continent, the Corps of Discovery aimed to show everyone who was in charge.

Blazing a Trail

Some have described the Lewis and Clark expedition as "the greatest camping trip of all time." It was a high adventure journey, no doubt. But in reality, the Corps of Discovery was the first scientific expedition funded by the United States government. Its success certainly blazed the trail for future exploration of the country's vast territory.

When Lewis and Clark headed west, the typical image of the western part of the continent looked very different from today. It likely pictured a rather empty interior and a single mountain range that served as the western continental divide.

Within about fifty years of Lewis and Clark's journey, more and more mapmakers and explorers followed in their footsteps. In the 1850s, the Army Corps of Topographical Engineers surveyed the United States' northwestern and southwestern boundaries. The map of the western part of the continent became much like the maps of today.

The botanical notes and specimens that Lewis and Clark sent back to Washington gave a jump start to the nation's scientific knowledge. They formed the basis for the first big scientific publication to illustrate and describe the plants found west of the Mississippi. The specimens became part of the permanent collection of the Academy of Natural Sciences in Philadelphia.

Pompey's Pillar

One lasting relationship established with the Native population was forged between Lewis and Clark and Sacagawea's son, Jean Baptiste "Pompy" Charbonneau. Clark enjoyed the boy so much he named a sandstone formation used as a landmark Pompy's Tower. It is now called Pompey's Pillar National Monument. Clark carved his name and the date, July 25, 1806, in the rock. The carving is the only on-site evidence of the expedition still visible.

Clark offered to adopt the boy after the expedition, and he was allowed by the child's father to do that in 1813, one year after Sacagawea's death. Young Pompy was educated in St. Louis and was taken to Europe, where he met members of the aristocracy and learned German and Spanish (he already spoke French, English, and two Native languages). Pompy returned to the United States and spent time on the frontier, as his father did. He lived an adventurous life and died at the age of sixty-one in Oregon.

Beginning of the End

Lewis and Clark tried to establish American control over the many lands and peoples of the Louisiana Territory (and beyond). By the time they set off on their journey of discovery, hundreds of **generations** of Native people had lived in the areas near the Missouri River. Many scholars say that the Corps of Discovery was successful because of what they learned along the way from Native Americans.

During their travels, Lewis and Clark did establish some friendly relationships with various Native American tribes throughout the continent. Writers Allen Pinkham and Steven Evans have written about the relations between the Corps of Discovery and the Nez Percés. They discuss how the Nez Percés and the expedition parted ways in July 1806 in Montana. They say, "For these young guides and the Nez Percé Nation, the time spent with the Corps of Discovery was over. The exploration team would be disbanded that fall (1806), but the association and alliance with the Americans was just beginning."

However, the Corps of Discovery did not make a great impression on all of the Native American tribes it encountered. For example, the clash with the Blackfeet led to some very bad feelings toward the United States. Years after the skirmish that left two Blackfeet warriors dead, the tribe ended up killing three former members of the Lewis and Clark expedition.

Looking at the westward expansion movement with a long-term view, many Native Americans saw the Lewis and Clark expedition as "the beginning of the end" for their people. As American settlers pushed farther and farther west, many of the ties between the Corps of Discovery and the Native peoples were broken. Some settlers considered the lands of the West to be theirs (the Americans') alone.

The belief in manifest destiny fueled both the settlement of the West and the removal of Native Americans from lands that the white settlers valued. Over time, the fate of Native Americans changed. Most tribes lost their power and independence. Some were pushed onto reservations. The nomadic lifestyles of other tribes had to change as white settlers longed to put down roots without sharing that land with the people who had been there long before. Many Native Americans also died from diseases brought by settlers, travelers, and others who came after Lewis and Clark.

Lewis and Clark and Exploring the Louisiana Purchase

William C. Reynolds and J. C. Jones created this 1856 map to show the comparative area of the slave states and Free States and the territory open to freedom or slavery by the repeal of the Missouri Compromise.

Slavery and the Missouri Compromise

An expansion of the territory that allowed slavery in the United States was another consequence of the Louisiana Purchase. At the time of the purchase, slavery was allowed to expand into the Mississippi River valley and Louisiana.

In 1820, a law known as the Missouri Compromise was passed. This law was passed to maintain the balance in Congress between Free States and slave states. Except for Missouri, the Missouri Compromise "prevented slavery in the Louisiana Territory north of the 36°30' **latitude** line," according to the Library of Congress website. This new law let Maine into the United States as a Free State and Missouri as a slave state.

As the nineteenth century continued, tension and hostility grew between Americans in favor of and against slavery. The Missouri Compromise was **repealed** in 1854 by the Kansas-Nebraska Act. Just three years later, the Supreme Court declared in the Dred Scott decision that the Missouri Compromise was unconstitutional, and that Congress was not allowed to prohibit slavery in the American territories. The disagreement over slavery and of the rights of states to make their own choice in the matter led to the Civil War in 1861.

New Adventures and Journals

After the Corps of Discovery disbanded in the fall of 1806, Meriwether Lewis was appointed governor of the Louisiana Territory. He died in 1809. William Clark held a variety of government posts. He became governor of the newly formed Missouri Territory in 1813. In 1822 he was named **superintendent** of Indian affairs. Clark died in 1838.

In thanks for their service, the US government gave each member of the Corps of Discovery (except for York) land. Lewis and Clark each got 1,600 acres (647 ha). The other members of the expedition received 320 acres (129 ha).

The journals of the Corps of Discovery made a long-lasting impact on the United States. These journals were not published right after the expedition because Lewis and Clark were busy with new endeavors. It was really after Lewis's death that Clark settled down to the business of getting their journals ready for publication. They were published in 1814.

In 1978, the National Park Service established the Lewis and Clark National Historic Trail. This trail connects eleven states and many Native American tribal lands. About 3,700 miles (5,955 km) long, it extends from Wood River, Illinois, to the mouth of the Columbia River in Oregon. Those who want to explore this region can follow in the footsteps of the Corps of Discovery, knowing the land has been preserved for generations of explorers to come.

Chronology

Dates in green pertain to events discussed in this volume.

September 28, 1542: Juan Rodríguez Cabrillo "discovers" present-day California. He claims the region for Spain.

February 1682: The French explorer René-Robert Cavelier, sieur de La Salle leads an expedition down the Mississippi River. He claims for France the territory drained by the Mississippi River from Canada to the Gulf of Mexico. He names this territory Louisiana.

October 1, 1800: France and Spain draw up the Treaty of San Ildefonso. This treaty transfers control of Louisiana, including the port of New Orleans, from Spain to France.

January 18, 1803: President Thomas Jefferson requests funding for an expedition to explore the American West.

April 30, 1803: The United States under President Jefferson buys 828,000 square miles (2.1 million square kilometers) of land west of the Mississippi River from France in a deal known as the Louisiana Purchase.

October 20, 1803: The US Senate ratifies the Louisiana Purchase Treaty.

November 30, 1803: Louisiana is officially transferred from Spanish control to French control.

December 20, 1803: France officially transfers Louisiana to the United States.

May 14, 1804: Meriwether Lewis and William Clark leave Camp DuBois with the Corps of Discovery to explore the Louisiana Purchase and try to find a water route to the Pacific coast.

August 20, 1804: Sergeant Charles Floyd dies of natural causes near modern-day Sioux City, Iowa. He is the only member of the expedition to die during the journey.

November 1804: Lewis and Clark meet the Shoshone woman Sacagawea and her French Canadian husband, Toussaint Charbonneau, in North Dakota. They are hired as guides and interpreters for the expedition.

December 24, 1804: The Corps of Discovery finishes building Fort Mandan in present-day North Dakota. They remain there for the entire winter.

June 13, 1805: The expedition arrives at the Great Falls of the Missouri River.

November 1805: The Corps of Discovery reaches the Pacific Ocean.

July 3, 1806: The Corps of Discovery splits into two groups. Lewis and some men set off to explore the Marais River. Clark and the rest of the team proceed to the Yellowstone River.

July 27, 1806: Meriwether Lewis and Reuben Field kill two members of the Blackfeet tribe in a skirmish.

August 12, 1806: Lewis's and Clark's parties reunite near Sanish, North Dakota.

September 23, 1806: The Lewis and Clark expedition makes it back to St. Louis, almost two and a half years after departing.

March 3, 1820: The Missouri Compromise passes, excluding slavery in territories of the Louisiana Purchase north of latitude 36°30', except Missouri.

December 2, 1823: President James Monroe declares that the American continents "are henceforth not to be considered as subjects for future colonization by any European powers." This principle would become known as the Monroe Doctrine. Along with manifest destiny, it supplies support for westward expansion.

May 28, 1830: President Andrew Jackson signs the Indian Removal Act, allowing for the removal of Native Americans from their homelands to unsettled land west of the Mississippi.

March 2, 1836: In the midst of a war with Mexico, Texas declares its independence from Mexico. The war ends with Texas becoming an independent territory. The issue of slavery delays its entry into the United States for nearly ten years.

May 22, 1843: A group of one thousand American settlers leaves from Independence, Missouri, by wagon train, heading over what would become known as the Oregon Trail to the Oregon Territory. A large-scale wave of westward migration follows.

July–August 1845: The term "manifest destiny" is coined by John L. O'Sullivan in an article on the annexation of Texas published in the *United States Magazine and Democratic Review*.

February 10, 1846: Members of the Church of Jesus Christ of Latter-Day Saints (Mormons) leave Illinois to escape persecution and head west for territory then controlled by Mexico. They settle in the valley of the Great Salt Lake in Utah.

April 25, 1846: The Mexican-American War, fought over the disputed border between Texas and Mexico, begins.

January 24, 1848: James Marshall discovers gold at John Sutter's mill in California.

February 2, 1848: Representatives from the United States and Mexico sign the Treaty of Guadalupe Hidalgo, ending the Mexican-American War and ceding more than 500,000 square miles (1.3 million sq km) to the United States.

September 9, 1850: California becomes the thirty-first state.

December 30, 1853: The United States buys 29,670 square miles (76,845 sq km) from Mexico in what is known as the Gadsden Purchase. The area later becomes part of Arizona and New Mexico.

May 30, 1854: Congress passes the Kansas-Nebraska Act, which overturns the Missouri Compromise and makes popular sovereignty the determining factor in allowing slavery to exist in a state.

May 20, 1862: President Abraham Lincoln signs the Homestead Act, which provides settlers 160 acres (65 hectares) of public land west of the Mississippi provided they live on the land for five consecutive years.

July 1, 1862: Congress passes the Pacific Railway Act, which aids in the construction of the transcontinental railroad from Council Bluffs, Iowa, to the Pacific coast. The railroad is built between 1863 and 1869.

May 10, 1869: Workers connect the Union Pacific and Central Pacific Railroads. Passengers can travel from New York to California in just eight days.

Glossary

amateur A person who takes part in an activity without payment; a nonprofessional.

botany The scientific study of plants.

conciliatory Intended or likely to calm a person or group.

continental The mainland section of the United States, not including Alaska or Hawaii.

council A meeting or assembly held for the purpose of consultation or advice.

delegation A body of representatives or delegates.

diplomacy The profession or activity of managing international relations, often through a country's representatives abroad.

diplomat An official who represents a country abroad (outside of that country).

Federalist An early political party in the United States.

generation A group of individuals born at about the same time.

intercept To block or obstruct someone in order to prevent him from continuing to a destination.

latitude The distance north or south of the equator, measured in degrees. Longitude is the distance east or west of the prime meridian, measured in degrees.

motive A reason for doing something, especially one that is not obvious.

pirogue A long canoe constructed from a single tree trunk.

ratify To give formal consent to a treaty or agreement, making it officially valid.

repeal To revoke or cancel a law or congressional act.

retroactively Taking effect from a date that is in the past, often used in terms of legislation.

sedentary Living in the same place throughout life; not nomadic or migratory.

sovereignty The authority of a state to govern itself or another state.

superintendent A person who manages or directs something.

tributaries Rivers or creeks that flow into and become part of a larger running body of water.

tribute Payment paid by one group or state to another, especially as a sign of dependence.

virtue Behavior that shows strong moral standards.

zoology The scientific study of animals.

Further Information

Books

Morley, Jacqueline. *You Wouldn't Want to Explore With Lewis and Clark!: An Epic Journey You'd Rather Not Make*. New York: Children's Press, 2013.

St. George, Judith. *What Was the Lewis and Clark Expedition?* New York: Grosset & Dunlap, 2014.

Stille, Darlene R. *The Journals of Lewis and Clark*. Chicago: Heinemann Library, 2012.

Yasuda, Anita. *12 Incredible Facts About The Louisiana Purchase*. North Mankato, MN: 12 Story Library, 2016

Websites

Kids Discover: The Louisiana Purchase Infographic
http://www.kidsdiscover.com/infographics/infographic-louisiana-purchase
In addition to featuring a great map, this website gives some history behind the Louisiana Purchase.

National Geographic: Go West Across America with Lewis and Clark
http://www.nationalgeographic.com/west
Travel across the country with Lewis and Clark in an interactive game where you help explorers make decisions.

PBS: Lewis and Clark
http://www.pbs.org/lewisandclark
Follow the expedition using interactive trail maps and to learn more about the Native American tribes Lewis and Clark met.

Bibliography

Books

Fleming, Thomas. *The Great Divide: The Conflict Between Washington And Jefferson That Defined a Nation*. Boston: Da Capo Press, 2015.

———. *The Louisiana Purchase*. Hoboken, NJ: John Wiley & Sons, Inc., 2003.

Hoxie, Frederick E., and Jay T. Nelson, eds. *Lewis & Clark and the Indian Country: The Native American Perspective*. Urbana: University of Illinois Press, 2007.

Josephy, Alvin M., Jr., ed. *Lewis and Clark Through Indian Eyes*. New York: Alfred A. Knopf, 2006.

Kastor, Peter J., ed. *The Louisiana Purchase: Emergence of an American Nation*. Washington, DC.: CQ Press, 2002.

Levinson, Sanford, and Bartholomew H. Sparrow, eds. *The Louisiana Purchase and American Expansion, 1803–1898*. Lanham, MD: Rowman & Littlefield, 2005.

Pinkham, Allen V., and Steven R. Evans. *Lewis and Clark Among the Nez Perce: Strangers in the Land of the Nimiipuu*. Washburn, ND: The Dakota Institute Press, 2013.

Online Articles

"After Lewis & Clark—Rivers, Edens, Empires: Lewis & Clark and the Revealing of America." Library of Congress. Retrieved November 14, 2016. https://www.loc.gov/exhibits/lewisandclark/lewis-after.html.

Allen, Michael. "The Federalists and the West 1783–1803." Portland State University. Retrieved November 16, 2016. https://journals.psu.edu/wph/article/download/3549/3380.

"Basic Information—Lewis & Clark National Historic Trail." National Park Service. Retrieved November 15, 2016. https://www.nps.gov/lecl/planyourvisit/basicinfo.htm.

"Captain Meriwether Lewis's Speech to the Yankton Sioux, August 30, 1804." National Park Service, Missouri National Recreational River. Retrieved November 14, 2016. https://www.nps.gov/mnrr/planyourvisit/upload/L&CSpeech.pdf.

"Continuing the Legacy of Lewis and Clark." USGS. Retrieved November 14, 2016. https://www2.usgs.gov/features/lewisandclark/factsheet2.pdf.

"Fort Mandan Winter." Discovering Lewis & Clark. Retrieved November 11, 2016. http://www.lewis-clark.org/article/1463.

Harriss, Joseph. "How the Louisiana Purchase Changed the World." *Smithsonian*, April 2003. http://www.smithsonianmag.com/history/how-the-louisiana-purchase-changed-the-world-79715124.

"The Journals of the Lewis and Clark Expedition." University of Nebraska–Lincoln. Retrieved November 14, 2016. http://lewisandclarkjournals.unl.edu.

"Lewis and Clark and the Nez Perce." National Park Service. Retrieved November 14, 2016. https://www.nps.gov/nepe/learn/historyculture/lewis-and-clark.htm.

"Lewis and Clark Expedition Discoveries and Tribes Encountered." National Geographic. Retrieved November 14, 2016. http://www.nationalgeographic.com/lewisandclark/resources_discoveries_tribe.html.

"Lewis & Clark Expedition: Scientific Encounters." National Park Service. Retrieved November 14, 2016. https://www.nps.gov/nr/travel/lewisandclark/encounters.htm.

"The Louisiana Purchase: Jefferson's Constitutional Gamble." National Constitution Center, October 20, 2016. http://blog.constitutioncenter.org/2016/10/the-louisiana-purchase-jeffersons-constitutional-gamble.

"Primary Documents in American History: Louisiana Purchase." Library of Congress. Retrieved November 9, 2016. https://www.loc.gov/rr/program/bib/ourdocs/Louisiana.html.

"Robert Livingston." Biography.com. Retrieved November 9, 2016. http://www.biography.com/people/robert-r-livingston-9383941#new-constitution-and-after.

Ronda, James P. "The Teton Confrontation." The Journals of the Lewis and Clark Expedition, University of Nebraska. Retrieved November 16, 2016. http://lewisandclarkjournals.unl.edu/read/?_xmlsrc=lc.ronda.01.02.xml&_xslsrc=LCstyles.xsl.

———. "Why Lewis and Clark Matter." Smithsonian, August 2003. http://www.smithsonianmag.com/history/why-lewis-and-clark-matter-87847931/?no-ist.

"Sergeant Patrick Gass." PBS. Retrieved November 11, 2016. http://www.pbs.org/lewisandclark/inside/pgass.html.

"Thomas Jefferson—Message to the Senate of January 11, 1803, Regarding Louisiana." The Avalon Project, Yale Law School. Retrieved November 10, 2016. http://avalon.law.yale.edu/19th_century/tj003.asp.

Index

Lewis and Clark and Exploring the Louisiana Purchase

About the Author

From circus science to jellybeans, **ALICIA KLEPEIS** loves to research fun and out-of-the-ordinary topics that make nonfiction exciting for readers. Alicia began her career at the National Geographic Society. She is the author of many children's books, including *Bizarre Things We've Called Medicine*, *Goblins*, *Understanding Saudi Arabia Today*, and *The World's Strangest Foods*. Her middle grade historical novel *A Time for Change* was released in 2016. She lives with her family in upstate New York, though she would love to retrace the steps of Lewis and Clark someday. And just like these explorers, she writes letters to people far away and keeps a journal.